Mega Military Machines™
Megamáquinas militares™

SUBMARINES

SUBMARINOS

Catherine Ellis

Traducción al español: María Cristina Brusca

PowerKiDS press & **Editorial Buenas Letras**™

New York

Published in 2007 by The Rosen Publishing Group, Inc.
29 East 21st Street, New York, NY 10010

First Edition

Editor: Amelie von Zumbusch
Book Design: Greg Tucker
Layout Design: Lissette González

Photo Credits: Cover © AFP/AFP/Getty Images; p. 5 © Phil Mislinski/Getty Images; p. 7 © Julian Herbert/Getty Images; p. 9 U.S. Navy file photo; p. 11 image copyright Daniel Gale, 2006. Used under license from Shutterstock, Inc.; p. 13 Department of Defense; p. 15 © Toru Yamanaka/AFP/Getty Images; p. 17 © China Photos/Getty Images; p. 19 by Mass Communication Specialist Seaman Joshua Martin, U.S. Navy; p. 21 by Journalist 1st Class Jason E. Miller, U.S. Navy; p. 23 by Petty Officer 2nd Class Steven H. Vanderwerff, U.S. Navy. Department of Defense.

Cataloging Data

Ellis, Catherine.
    Submarines / Catherine Ellis; traducción al español: María Cristina Brusca. — 1st ed.
        p. cm. — (Mega military machines–Megamáquinas militares)
    Includes index.
    ISBN-13: 978-1-4042-7620-8 (library binding)
    ISBN-10: 1-4042-7620-3 (library binding)
    1. Submarines (Ships)—Juvenile literature. 2. Spanish language materials I. Title.

Manufactured in the United States of America

Contents

Submarines 4

Submarines and the Navy 10

How Submarines Work 18

Words to Know 24

Index 24

Contenido

Submarinos 4

Submarinos en la armada 10

Cómo funcionan
los submarinos 18

Palabras que debes saber 24

Índice 24

Submarines are boats that can go underwater. They can dive down as deep as 1,600 feet (488 m).

Los submarinos son barcos que pueden navegar por debajo del agua. Se pueden sumergir hasta 1,600 pies (488 m) de profundidad.

The people who work on military submarines are part of the navy.

Las personas que trabajan en los submarinos militares forman parte de la marina de guerra.

Submarines are very big. You can see their full size only when they are on dry land to be fixed or cleaned, though.

Los submarinos son muy grandes. Sólo puedes ver todo su tamaño cuando los sacan del agua para limpiarlos o repararlos.

The navy uses submarines to watch ships from unfriendly countries secretly.

La armada usa submarinos para vigilar en secreto a los barcos de los países enemigos.

A submarine's shape lets it move easily through the water.

Los submarinos tienen una forma especial. Ésto les permite moverse con facilidad en el agua.

Submarines often move slowly so that they make little noise. However, they can go as fast as 29 miles per hour (47 km/h).

Muchas veces, los submarinos se mueven lentamente para hacer poco ruido. Pero también pueden navegar muy rápido, hasta 29 millas por hora (47 km/h.).

The navy uses submarines to fire **missiles**. Submarines can even fire missiles when they are underwater.

La marina usa submarinos para disparar **misiles**. Los submarinos pueden disparar misiles debajo del agua.

Submarines have a **periscope**. A periscope lets you see what is going on outside of the submarine.

Los submarinos tienen periscopios. Con el **periscopio** se puede ver lo que sucede fuera del submarino.

Submarines have big **propellers**. A submarine's propellers spin to move the boat through the water.

Los submarinos tienen grandes **hélices.** Las hélices giran para impulsarlo en el agua.

Some submarines can come up through a big sheet of ice!

¡Algunos submarinos pueden salir a la superficie rompiendo grandes capas de hielo!

Words to Know / Palabras que debes saber

missiles (MIH-sulz) Things that are shot at something far away.

periscope (PER-ih-skohp) A tool that is used to see above the top of the water from underwater.

propellers (pruh-PEL-erz) Paddlelike parts on an object that spin to move the object forward.

---

hélices (las) Las aspas que giran para mover un objeto.

misiles (los) Objetos que se disparan a un lugar lejano.

periscopio (el) Instrumento para ver sobre la superficie del agua cuando el submarino está sumergido.

Index

B
boat(s), 4, 20

N
navy, 6, 10, 16

S
shape, 12
size, 8

W
water, 12, 20

Índice

A
agua, 12, 20
armada, 6, 10, 16

B
barco(s), 4, 20

F
forma, 12

T
tamaño, 8